Who are you?

In the
Rainforest

Vic Parker and Ross Collins

W
FRANKLIN WATTS
LONDON•SYDNEY

I'm a stripy hunter, padding
silently on big paws.
I wait and watch. Then I…

Who
are
you?

I perch up high and peck at fruit.
Then I flap my wings and fly.
To talk I...

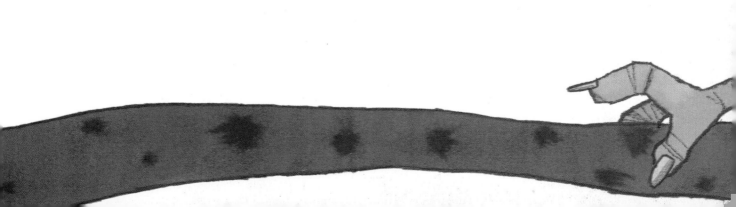

I lie low in the water like
a lumpy log, webbed feet
paddling, strong tail swishing.
My toothy jaws open wide
and I…

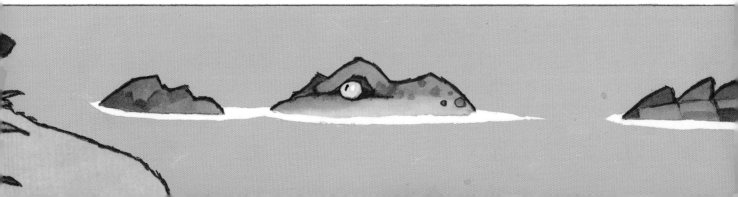

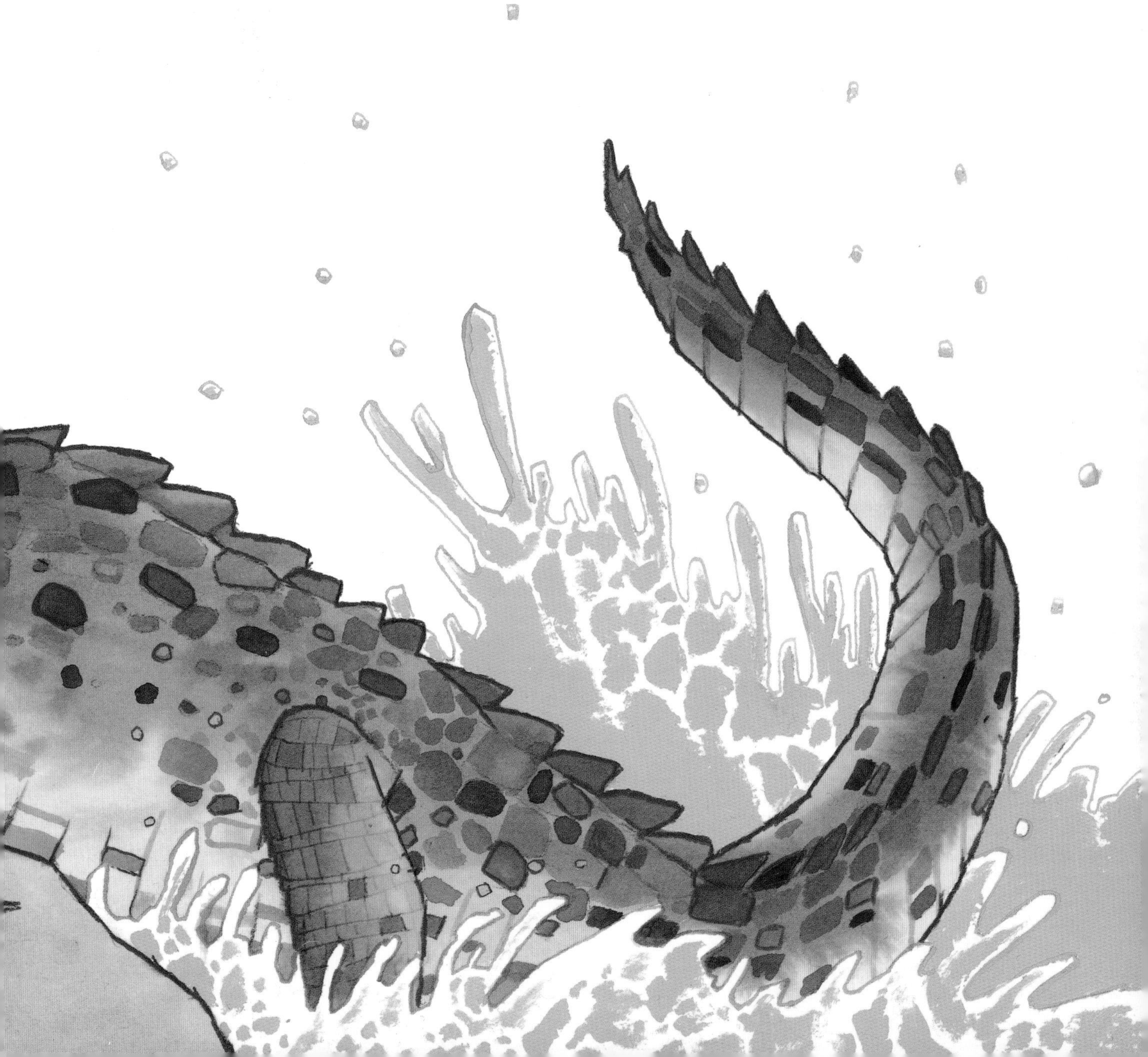

I live high in the trees climbing with my furry hands and feet. I've got extra long arms to help me…

We all live in the rainforest.

Tiger

Chameleon

Crocodile

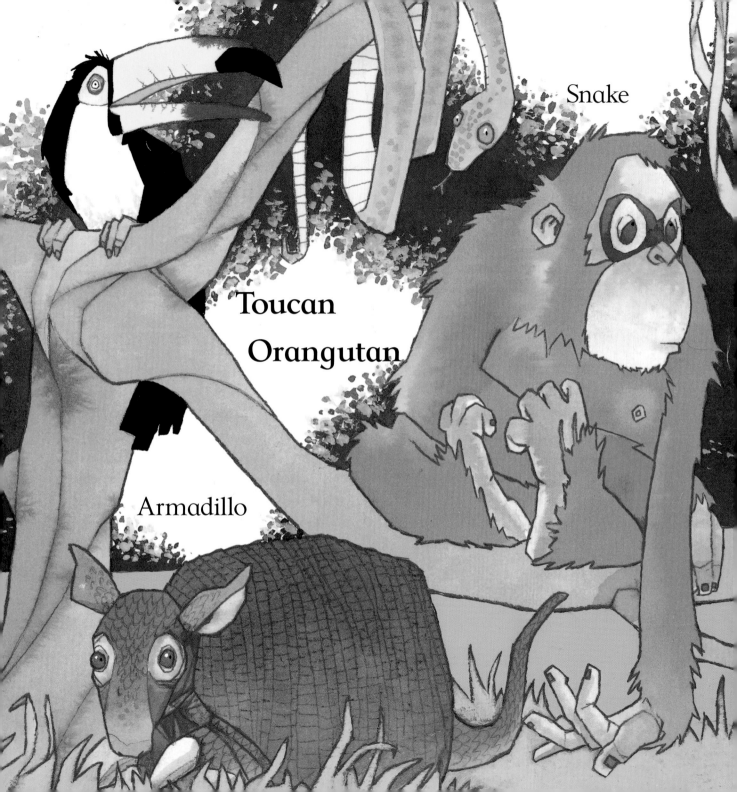

Snake

Toucan

Orangutan

Armadillo

Sharing books with your child

Me and My World is a range of books for you to share with your child. Together you can look at the pictures and talk about the subject or story. Listening, looking and talking are the first vital stages in children's reading development, and lay the early foundation for good reading habits.

Talking about the pictures is the first step in involving children in the pages of a book, especially if the subject or story can be related to their own familiar world. When children can relate the matter in the book to their own experience, this can be used as a starting point for introducing new knowledge, whether it is counting, getting to know colours or finding out how other people live.

Gradually children will develop their listening and concentration skills as well as a sense of what a book is. Soon they will learn how a book works: that you turn the pages from right to left, and read the story from left to right on a double page. They start to realise that the black marks on the page have a meaning and that they relate to the pictures. Once children have grasped these basic essentials they will develop strategies for "decoding" the text such as matching words and pictures, and recognising the rhythm of the language in order to predict what comes next. Soon they will start to take on the role of an independent reader, handling and looking at books even if they can't yet read the words.

Most important of all, children should realise that books are a source of pleasure. This stems from your reading sessions which are times of mutual enjoyment and shared experience. It is then that children find the key to becoming real readers.

This edition 2004

Franklin Watts
96 Leonard Street,
London EC2A 4XD

Franklin Watts Australia
45-51 Huntley Street
Alexandria NSW 2015

ISBN 0 7496 5650 6

A CIP catalogue record for this book is available from the British Library
Dewey Classification 649

First published in the Early Worms series

Printed in Belgium

Consultant advice: Sue Robson and Alison Kelly,
Senior Lecturers in Education,
Faculty of Education, Early Childhood Centre,
Roehampton Institute, London.